I thought of you last night

WRITINGS BY
Jehan Saleh

Writing Contribution & Illustration by
Raiyan A. Berry

Edited by Mary L. Eastland

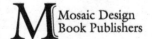

Mosaic Design
Book Publishers

I thought of you last night

Copyright 2017 Jehan Saleh

First Printing – August 2017

ISBN: 978-0-9968933-6-7 *(paperback)*
ISBN: 978-0-9968933-7-4 *(eBook)*

Printed in the United States of America on acid-free paper.

Published by Mosaic Design Book Publishers
Dearborn, Michigan USA

0 1 2 3 4 5 6 7 8 9

This book is dedicated to the ones I love.

God, for everything.

My beloved son, Raiyan,
for inspiring me to be everything God wants me to be.
You have given me reason to live and you are the love in my life.

My father, Sam, and mother, Fay.
Both of you are pillars of strength and forces of light illuminating
my path and guiding me along my way.

You are trailblazers ~ You taught me how to fly,
rise above and remain rooted while living life.
Through you, I learned to be the best version of myself.

You believed in me and taught me to reach for the moon
and fall upon the stars.

My brothers, Kain, David and Robert, and my sister, Nessrine,
for being everything I could ever want them to be
and loving me unconditionally.

My cousin Steven for making me smile.

So fortunate and blessed to have walked the distance with you.

For you, with love,
Jehan

INTRODUCTION

Come and visit with Jehan Saleh. Look into her mind, her heart and yes, her very soul as she converses with herself and others along her life's journey.

The passion, the pain, the joy, the ecstasy…it's all there. You will find a young woman who is in touch with her own thoughts and feelings to the end that she inadvertently invites you into her life with every word.

You will find a young woman who listens to her soul as it leads her to the knowledge that we are one people, all alike though all different.

You will find a young woman who seeks God where He may be found which, as she understands, is everywhere, in each and every one of His creations. She is not hesitant to give praise to our Creator, not embarrassed to acknowledge Him yet not saccharine in her accolades.

You will find a young woman who is not afraid to acknowledge her own doubts, her own fears, her own passions. And she is indeed a passionate, beautiful young woman who is equally as grounded, level-headed, and rational as she is whimsical.

You will find a young woman who is passionately seeking love and is capable and wholeheartedly willing to return love.

Come and visit with Jehan. It is a visit you will not forget, one that will tweak your own passions and return in your own thoughts well into your future.

Mary L. Eastland

I thought of you last night

I Am In Love

I was lying in my bed for sake of peace of mind
And you suddenly popped into my thoughts.
Doesn't it feel terribly awkward talking on the phone with one another?
It's sort of like an uncomfortable feeling that cannot be understood.
Although, I must say, it's always exciting after I hang up the phone. Why?
You rewind time.
You take me back in time to an unexplainable
Walk I took along this journey of life.

So…
I miss your intellect and depth.
I want to recapture that strange electricity
I felt when your energy intertwined with mine.
I know there are things that cannot be written down but
Write me quickly for fear of losing that forever.
I want some more.

Once upon a time. Oh time…it's been so long since I felt you.

For Mom
From Me

Your eye is a star that shines above,
Your hair is a rainbow that glitters around your head,
Your body is the sun that shines in the day,
Your voice is the moon that gives light to the light.

Raiyan Berry

Trees…

A Sin or Worse

I can't imagine why I cannot feel these feelings. It's like a sudden crash.
While your emotions painfully stroke your insides
Commotion grows within you and around you.
It is enough to make you cry.

"The best and most beautiful things in the world
cannot be seen or even touched.
They must be felt with the heart."
— *Helen Keller*

Quiet

Even Though

I know you called me
Even before I wrote to you last.

Why don't I want to write? Allow me to introduce myself to you.

Consideration for other people is a quality that many human beings lack
Due to the natural, innate selfishness we all possess.
When a considerate person walks into my life I treasure them.
So, when you're considerate enough to respond to my e-mail
I will be considerate enough to shower you with my delicious words.

Never the less, even though you did not respond
To my e-mail I wrote to you.
I guess it's just that natural kindness or 'whatever' I possess.

I'm glad you're enjoying Paris.
I hope you're happy there since you are there.

You know, if there is one thing in this world I lack knowledge of
It is politics.
I don't like politics or politicians!
They go hand in hand in destroying the balance of the world
And human rights.
I may be wrong.

May I?

is of

Philosophically speaking...

War. War occurs when one party wants something from another party
And will not stop fighting until there is an exchange.

Therefore,
The burden of compromise lies on Israel
Because Palestine has nothing to give.
Israel has taken everything:
Land...homes...irrigation...water...pride...dignity...respect...
human rights.

SO, if in fact Israel really wants peace, it is up to them!
But I don't think they want peace.
I just think they want the entire land of Palestine.

It's sort of like the social exchange theory...
In order to have a healthy relationship or balance of some sort
Both sides must receive something from the other
Whether it be respect, love, admiration, land, water.
There is nothing to give Israel and this is why peace is difficult to achieve.
And, if there is peace
How sad it will be...
Palestinians living in poverty.

Regardless, this is why I don't know much about politics. I choose not to!

I'm starting to miss you less.

the mind.

That's not a great thing. Actually, it's saddening.
It's as frustrating for me
As it is frustrating for you.
I don't know why human beings like torturing themselves.
I guess it's the social exchange theory again.
So, what is it that you get from me?
Can't you find it somewhere else?

Anyway, there are times when I just fall into a daze thinking of you.
I'm anxious for your arrival my love
So we can walk in the park,
So we can go to a symphony,
So we can do all the different things
Life brings.
I'm excited over your arrival (soon is not soon enough)
So I can explore you,
So I can watch you,
So I can admire you.
I am in wonder of you!

There are times when I don't want to think of you.
What's the point?

Serenity

Only You

The mere thought of your words is enough to wake me from my dreams
As do my words to you.
I take pleasure and pay attention to your every word.
They are a part of the brilliant you.

You're empty inside
Because you're sooooo brilliant.

feels

What Is Underneath

How do you feel about not living in your homeland?
You have some strong ethical and moral values within yourself, don't you!

I was at an interview the other day and I was asked,
"What is the one thing that nobody can change about you?"
I had to search deep within my heart for that answer
Because I believe in compromise.
Human beings are all different.
We're all wired in our own way.
That's what makes God so Godly.
But, there is one thing that nobody can change about me…
My ethical values, morals, and beliefs.
I'm rather strong, firm and grounded
When it comes to my spirituality and God.
For example, as I was kissing you I thought to myself,
"Does God know why I am kissing him?"
As I thought about it a little, I closed my eyes a little tighter and thought,
"Yes, God understands. He knows I reserve myself. He knows that I
Must feel a complete energy balance with this man, spiritually, mentally,
Physically, and emotionally to even allow him into my world.
Yes, I think God understands."

kind.

Crazy

I just finished getting all dolled up, Darling.
I clothed myself with my faux fur coat
And some vintage clothes I picked up;
Covered my eyes in black;
Wet my lips for comfort;
Colored my cheeks in a girly-girl pink;
Painted my nails messy
And spiked my hair to crazy angles.

I'm going to the theatre with simply sparkling me.
I feel crazy about me
Being all 'glamoured' up.
It's almost time for the show.
"Dancer in the Dark", don't dance without me.

The Universe

Peace Negotiations

Sometimes, I want a response from you.
Sometimes, I don't bother myself thinking of it.
It's truth…you know…just truth.

is a

Calling Your Name

I was driving today in my beetle
When a powerful thought of you flashed through me.
So I decided to write for the sake of my thoughts.
Tell me about you.
I know what I must know
But oh how I wish you would
Tell me about the little things.
Do you like ice cream?
What makes you smile?
Do you like operas?

ribcage

Us

Are you understanding?

I mean, can you really understand another person;
their energy, their voice,
their body, their movements, their words,
the fact that they are human beings?

Do you understand that the person sitting across from you
is not your brother, rather,
he's a human being?

of His

Protective

I'm very protective of my soul, heart, conscience, being, spirit, skeleton.
To know me is to know my need for understanding.

And yes,
I could have, would have, but did not.
The thought, "Should have", did not cross my mind.
See, there were other things on my mind,
Other people demanding my time.

I never thanked you for your admiration.
Thank you for admiring every inch of me.
For seeing all the beauty outside of me.
For touching the beauty living inside of me.
For awakening so many specialties hidden within me.
It's an unexplainable intangible you give me.
More than just realization.

Whatever comes will come. But don't stray for more than ten days.
It's a pity when you leave for too long.

dimension,

As for my baby, Bella,

All that's left is an empty space.

It was so easy giving all my love without being scared to give it.

It was fulfilling receiving all of her unconditional love.

"To love is something,

To be loved is another thing,

To love and be loved is everything."

It brought a smile when my eyes watched her. I literally saw me in her.

They say puppies take on their owners personality and she really did.

She took on the child in me. She was so happy, wild, free, playful, smart,

Adventurous, loving, prissy and just exploring everything around her.

My father told me that she drove him crazy the first week I was gone.

I asked him what she did to make him mad.

He said, "She kept ripping the toilet paper all over the place."

I began to cry and choking on my words I softly said, "Baba, she wanted

Attention, that's all, she just wanted your attention. She was lonely."

He said, "Oh well, I was busy."

I was driving through the streets and I asked a man if he spotted a little

Puppy Shih Tzu and he said, "No." He asked me how I lost her.

I said I was overseas and I left her with my brothers and father.

He said, "Oh, she must have been trying to find home."

I know she was. I know she was trying to find me (home)

And I wasn't there for her.

She needed my presence, my attention and I failed her. It never failed,

When I would open the French doors to this house I would see her

Running full speed around the corner hallway to kiss and hug me "HI".

Imagine that little cute thing running full speed ahead to kiss and love

you "Hi".

I am on a spiral downward without her.

I need to get over this quickly.

A correlation,

Where Have All The Children Gone

I understand how natural it is to read something into everything.
But,
Don't read too far into some things...words, people.
Sometimes it can lead to assuming what may not really be there.
It's also very frustrating for the other person as well.
You can take my words at face value for what they're worth
Or don't take them at all.

Last night I went out with my friends.
A girl came with us, a seventeen year old girl.
I thought to myself, "She shouldn't be here.
She doesn't need to be seeing all of this so soon.
She's learning too many things too young.
She should take her time in growing up."
The sooner you learn about life, the sooner
Your child-like innocence is stripped away.

The more we grow, the more complicated it all becomes.
The more we learn, the harder the struggle to hold on
To that child-like innocence. Sometimes I think,
"It's sad to learn. I'm scared. I'm beside myself."

a reflection,

My little cousin came over the other day
Because she needed help with a love letter.
After I read the letter I wrote down four questions
And requested she give me a one sentence response to each of them.
She called me up this morning and read her answers.

You helped me learn about myself.
You show love by fear.
You like me and love me.
Isn't it wonderful to feel free.

I nearly curled up in a ball to the narrative of the last line,
"Isn't it wonderful to feel free."

I miss my puppy!

a monument

Giving Without Receiving

I'm all right though I feel terribly sick.
I think it's this stripping feeling I have within me.
It's making everything foggy.
I feel much better now, though.
My tummy is barely hurting me anymore.
My heart does not ache nearly half as much as before.
Time…I'm always fighting it. I have to let it play its role.
It's healing me. It does a great deal more that I failed to recognize before.
No?

I received your sexy message. I was like, "Wow" I want to hear that again.
So I replayed your voice. Then I thought,
"Geez I hope my father didn't hear this."
Then I realized, my father is not going to think it's sexy.
That's how I hear you.
He'll hear you differently. They will all hear you differently.

So, I wish you had left your number.
I wish we could share one another before this all wears off.
Do you think it will wear off soon?
I think with the distance between us, sadly, it probably will, I guess.
It's so unfair sometimes.
You are the closest thing to transparency in subtle, narrow ways.

of Him.

Waiting Anxiously

I have not yet heard from you.
I so want to speak with you before you leave my side of the world.
I want to meet you somewhere halfway.
I want you to play with me, talk to me, make-believe with me.
I want to play with you, talk to you, make-believe with you.
Don't you need to feel fulfilled for one moment?

Everything

Read Through To The Bottom

For the record,
I'm a romantic.
Yes, I do love love.

But the questions and answers of Adam and Eve hold deeper secrets.
So I ask,
"Why was Adam kicked out of the Heaven of God?"
Eve gave comfort to his eyes
And comfort to his soul.
What does this really mean?
It means so many different things.

Today, I realized that
Emotionally I am being challenged!
I don't like work.
Something is missing over there.
It's making things more clear.
I cannot have them suck my blood, my happiness.

is unified,

I need inspiration through
My surroundings,
My sensations,
My supernatural self,
My people,
My universe.
Being a novelist would be good for me or
Maybe someone like Socrates or
Shakespeare or both.
Ultimately, I want to work around my life and time.

And, I leave you with this…

You intellectualize everything
And everything can always be intellectualized.
Sometimes,
Don't you think, "Be careful."?
Sometimes,
Don't you think, "I'm brilliant!"?
And, all the time don't you think,
"If we knew the answers to everything,
There would be no such thing as God."
Tell me that you're smiling.

even

Last One, It's Fun

When you're driving in the car make it fun to be driving in the car.

Put the music on.
Don't evaluate yourself.
It's not terribly wrong for you to have fun with yourself in the car
So long as you keep it real.
Anyway,
Put the music on.
Be careful not to listen to slow music.
Psychologically I think it can make you depressed.

But, don't quote me. I have no experience with slow songs.
It must be true, though. I'm a human being, too.
Let the music take you there.
Pick up some music that has that beat,
A song that will make your
Insides crazy, your heart beat,
Your stomach sizzle and blood twist,
A song that will make you smile.
If you don't have music like this what a shame.

Music is sensational for the soul, simply wonderful, just beautiful.

the outside.

The Love of Night

Look at everything around you.
Focus in on one image that captures you
Like clouds in the sky.
Separate the clouds from the sky
But keep the sky there as your back-drop.
Isn't the world a painted picture,
A world in paintings?

See

Ever told your child,
"We'll do it tomorrow"
And in your haste,
Not see his sorrow?
Ever lost touch,
Let a good friendship die
Cause you never had time
To call and say, "Hi"?
You'd better slow down.
Don't dance so fast.
Time is short.
The music won't last.
When you run so fast to get somewhere
You miss half the fun of getting there.
When you worry and hurry through your day,
It's like an unopened gift thrown away.
Life is not a race.
Do take it slower.
Hear the music before the song is over.

A Little Girl Dying Somewhere

the trees

Speaking

I know we will speak later on tonight.
We will probably be speaking for a long time.
But...
While time breezes
Let's not miss out on the feeling of it's winds.

For some reason
I enjoy writing things to you.
It tickles me, it really does.

Your sister answered the phone today.
I hope you laugh all day today.

And...
Dance with your sister before you leave her.
Really look at her and dance with her.
Dance in the depth of her eyes
And the depth of her heart.

If you do so, you will dance with her soul.
Dance as if nothing in the world matters.
Dance as if nothing in the past ever happened.
Just make an exchange of something.

It's important.

He gives

Be sure not to forget about you little nephew. You told me he loves you.
Young men at his age don't really know what to make of things.

I don't know if he's emotional but if he's not
Help him take the plunge into his pool of emotions.
You will make him a better person,
More well-rounded, No?

I know it is not good to give advice but I'm not advising you,
I'm just reminding you!
It shouldn't be so complicated.

so we

Satisfaction Equals Relief

God is close to me. I feel He has always been.
When I was a little girl I used to write Him letters
and put them in my Holy Book.
I used to look up in the sky and talk to Him. I still do.
I feel choked with happiness, gratitude, admiration, fascination, love,
and oneness with everything surrounding me,
everything He created around me.

breathe.

Character

I'm not clever. This word goes against my very being.
But only he would
misunderstand things
without knowing they go misunderstood.

The trees

Power of His Mind

Oh, it's disappointing. I was hoping he would intellectually stimulate me by the written words of his thoughts. After all, it was his mind that told me, "Stay," not his physique.

create

Please Come

Feed me.
Feed me what we should always feed one another,
Transparency of the soul.

Find me.
Speak to me as I speak to you then we can play on the swings
Swinging high in the sky. And as you begin to fly,
The wind's velvet touch strokes your skin
And your stomach starts to tingle within you.

I shouldn't have written you last.
I was too within myself. I didn't really want to write you.
I should have continued in my serenity.
I needed to "fall inside of me" and nobody else.

But, I wrote to you.

What secrets would I find if I were to explore within you?

I don't feel like this anymore.

We were dancing a dance.
I could not help but smile.
You danced to me, with me, all around me.

gardens

I just came down from my sister's bedroom.
I woke her from her sleep.
I sat on her bed,
Leaned forward interrupting her dreams and
Felt that reckless gathering of emotions
And whispered to her,
"You want to be somebody?
Be somebody or you'll never be. And you're too
Precious not to be, Nesrine.
God said you would be."
I fell into shock and disappeared from there.

Wow!!!!! How your perception of 'Somebody' alters through the years.

There's something in me…in you.

You're losing me.

What are these millions of thoughts that enter the head everyday?

I randomly opened the Holy Book and read that

The relationship between a man and a woman can never be permanent.
It is only temporary and can at any moment be lost.

for us

So, it's a little like gardening, requiring attention
Twenty-four hours a day, seven days a week.
Either it becomes permanent because of you or it dies because of you.

But, we are so much more than this.
There is no other creation like the human being and its functioning.

Find me.

Fascinating! Wow!

How are you feeling today
With this talk of peace?
Did you watch the birds eating lunch?
It seems as if you like cafés (???).
Go to one that's far from all the noise
Or close to all the noise and get lost.
Fall inside yourself.

I have to go.

to see.

Dying

I'm dying to talk to him.
I'm dying to see him.
I'm dying to hear from him.
I'm dying to watch him.
I'm dying to touch him.
How great this feels.
Doesn't it?

See

Stimulation

I awoke this morning feeling exceptionally great
And I was just prancing around.
Not a person disrupted me.

We were in your room when you said to me, "Wow you're like a
Whirlwind of energy." I say, "It was your energy, too."
It was Friday evening when we bumped into one another and I said,
"So you like change." I say, "Life in all its stages is a whirlwind of change."

It was when you said, "I want to get to know you less."
I say, "Less is more."
It was as if we both just knew. I say, "Intuition does not
Come as easily as it did when we were strangers."

Do you recall when you told me, "I saw you around ten times today."?
I said, "You did? Where?" You said, "At brunch.
When the doors swung open a force made me turn around
And there you were with your glasses.
What's up with those glasses?"

the glaciers

"Well, for the record,
I, too, made direct contact with you, but I quickly turned my face
For fear of the unexplainable situation. I mean,
Of all the tables, of all the people, of all the noise, I only saw you.
There you were with this little halo of light surrounding you.
Your arm was on the chair, your body was turned,
And you had a smile on your face,
Just for the record."

So, utter passion…what do you think of it?
Passion that interrupts your world with arrogance; passion that disrupts
Your ever-changing world; passion that makes you think about
Your world. How do you feel about your passion?
Is it possible to be crazy for your passion?
Do you believe in love, or is it lust and commonality,
Or is it all none or both?

Imagine the fist kiss with any lady. Imagine the kiss being so intense
That it causes you to think, "Wow it's as if we've kissed for years."
Has this ever happened to you?
Could this ever happen to just anyone?

Once upon a time there was this alluring brown-eyed girl
And this captivating black-eyed beauty.

melt

Angry

So, you want to devour me? Lick me to the bone?

Here are my feelings about this situation I am in with you:
I've got a lover up in outer space.
He's been tumbling around
All over the place.
I like to call him from time to time.
We can talk about heaven,
Break away those ties?

Here is what my soul hungers for:
I need someone to catch each breath
That issues from my lips.
I need someone to get into my head.
I need someone to kiss.
I want to be your baby doll.

Here is how I look at things in general:
I don't care if you won't talk to me.
You know I'm not that kind of girl.
And I don't care if you won't walk with me.
It doesn't give me such a thrill.
And I don't care about the way you look.
You should know I'm not impressed
Because, well, there are too many reasons.

down

Here is what I think of you:
Truth is bothersome.
Something is missing somewhere.
Intriguing you are,
Handling people with correct care.
Moving too fast
To ever be satisfied.
Working too focused
To really indulge.
Misunderstanding things
Without really knowing they go misunderstood.

I once met a lion,
A caged lion.
He looked so serene and beautiful yet,
As lions are, ferocious and strong.
He was just great.

Here is what I feel about you:
Sometimes I feel like I have to take care of you
Which means that I need to be sure that you're happy.
Sometimes I feel like being your friend
But then, I already am.
Sometimes I feel like I can bask in this forever
Then again, you can burn if basking for too long.
I get so excited
Whenever I choose to think of you.
You're that fabulous to me.
You scare me.

their mountainsides

Anyway,
Habibi…Handsome; My tantalizing Freak of Nature;
Selfishly Satisfying; Tasty; Intellectually Stimulating,

You know what my soul hungers for.
I want to be somebody's treasured toy.

You know how I think of certain things in general.
I can really care less or more depending on the situation.

You know my thoughts of you.
I would rather think of you than not think of you at all.
It doesn't matter either way.
I have to be fair to me
Just as you have to be fair to you.
So tell me, really,
What do you want from me besides the awesome thought
Of munching on one another?

You can completely understand the predicament I am in.
I would like to just end this torture for myself.

Into rivers,

Autumn

Bonjour Cherri!

I was thinking of this question he asked me,
On which I stumbled.
He asked, "Why do you think I am so brilliant?"
It's rather difficult to make sense of my senses at times.
You see it's not something I am certain about.
It's something that I feel and sense.
Therefore, I will go with what my senses tell me.
They're usually right.
So, why do I think You are so brilliant?

From the kidney you shared with your brother
To this certain loyalty you have for your homeland,
To the respect you have earned for yourself by yourself,
To the noble cause you dedicate your days to,
And the power of the brain you choose to use rather than ignore,
I've never really met with brilliance like this before.
I just think you're a good person.

As I was lying in bed listening to the crickets singing their nightly tune
And feeling the breeze of Autumn too soon,
I thought of things…life, me, etc.
I closed my eyes and thought,
"I wonder about his cute curly black hair?"

into

There we were in that moment.
I tried running my fingers through his hair
But there was too much hair spray in it!
So I decided to touch it softly.
As I was admiring his hair
My eyes came across his forehead so I touched it.
And I wanted to kiss it as I would kiss a baby.
How I regret not kissing his forehead.
Regardless,
I shall not live in the lethargy of regrets.
I shall just march forward and never look back
Unless I choose to do so!

seas.

Small Talk

Everybody has something to say. So say it!
Every word that comes out of a persons mouth teaches me something,
Calms curiosity,
Tingles emotions,
Cures the craving for knowledge.
Learning sort of protects you, don't you think?
Learning is survival.
Learning, in essence, is the brain begging, yearning for more and more.
It is the wanting of enrichment. It can be as simple as a strange color
Fascinating to the human eye.

I learned something new today.
I'm a romantic,
An angel, and this world hardens me.
I was not meant to be hardened and this is good!

I asked a male acquaintance to tell me about, well, love!

Love is the most complex of all emotions
mostly because it is linked to sex.
You can have sex without love and you can have love without sex,
but too many people get confused about what they actually feel,
thus the divorce rate.

See

The desire for sex is so strong that it makes people do things they wouldn't normally do. It interferes with love in a way, because you may think you love someone but you only love their body parts.
So sex gets in the way and it's hard
to separate it from love.
But you have to learn to separate it before you can find true love.
Women tend to want to love someone first and then try to intensify
the bond with sex.
To most women, sex is the way that the closeness is kept.
On the other hand, men look for sex first and hope that love will follow.
Men think that a woman proves her love by giving him sex
and he proves his love
by taking care of her either financially or physically.

Wow! Isn't it exhilarating to learn sometime.
It puts things into perspective.
It brings understanding. You're better able to comprehend the person
you are and the person you have to be in order to survive,
in order to save yourself, your soul.
In this instance, I'm not every woman.
I just learned about the majority of them.
In this instance, I learned how some men or the majority of men
view certain subjects.

Share all of your experiences because as sad as learning can be,
it is just as wonderful.

You're a teacher of many experiences are you not?
I wish someone would tell me what I should be expecting in life.

the sky

Chemistry

All you sinners, stop wasting all the wonderful meanings of life.

Forgive us God, for we have sinned.
We have taken our prayers and turned them into passions.
Is passion not found in prayer?
Is prayer not passion?
Is passion not found in life?
Is life not passion?
Is conviction not found in both?

It's hard to compete with
Disaster - prayer in disaster,
Conflict - passion in conflict,
Sadness - pain in sadness,
Emotions - conviction in emotions.

These sensations are equal and opposite in life's 'life spectrum'.
Together they make up a chemistry that shakes you, moves you.

These questions you should philosophize on,
Just philosophize.
You're good at this, aren't you?
"The answers are within".

taking up

There we were kissing a kiss.
You said, "It feels like we've been kissing for years."
There we were, it seems haunting, with A Strange Kiss In Our Eyes.

In case you lose me
Read a wonderfully thought out book.
I'm sure you will find me there, somewhere, maybe.

Once upon a time, how fulfilling time can be.

Call somebody you love like your mommy
and exchange your love with one another.
It will make everything disappear as you fall into her voice.
Smile just to smile so you can release the chemical serotonin in your brain.
It is healthy for you because it keeps you happy.
Bonne journee

our

If You Are Who I Think You Are

If you are who I think you are…
At least you think you understand who I am.
How unfair am I?

My friend,
Tell me and I forget,
Show me and I remember,
Involve me and I understand.

We are all eternal students of life.
Some people just get caught up in the matrix of it.
Tomorrow will be a beautiful day.
It's a shame when one allows it to slip away.
So caught up in the chaos of things,
Giving no time for the invisible wonders God brings,
Lost in everything in the world but He.
If the world was perfect it would not be.

Yes, my friend,
Tomorrow will be a beautiful day and you will not let it get away
Depending on what your definition of beauty is,
Depending on how you embrace it to stay.

Creatures of Conquest…
We can barely conquer ourselves let alone one another.

I do miss your beauty, the beauty of you.

Truly, very truly…

water

Folding

How are you over there? Be careful.

If I ask you, will you come for me, love me and never let go?

Emotions…
Give me something to feed off of.
Tell me, show me, involve me.
It's your spirit that gives me breathe, life.

The taking…
Take, take, and take. I will give all the energy I have except my spirit.

In the end…
You can grasp the beauty of me for a quick fix of self-reliance,
Convenience, lifestyle, personality, and ego.
Timelessness is time, is God's gift.
But, in the end….

Tuesdays with Morrie…
Will you please read it for your personal growth and well-being?
It's short, one hour.

You're saving the world, your people, the chaos, yourself. Are you?
And so, what of your ego?

How better is it to learn from the Universe
than at the hand of one of God's own.
Human Beings…What we value are our insecurities.
Who are we?

To prevent

Masked within the four walls lies your spirit, your soul, Habibi.
Look at the reflection of yourself in the mirror.
Look at the 'Invisible Being' within you.
Look past your body into the heart of it all.
Selfishness is ignoring one's own soul.

How is your masterpiece coming along?
How will you publicize your book?
You can do lots:
Create a controversial web-site and e-mail the web site address
to all Arabs and Israelis;
There is on-line shopping;
You can also hire a PR firm to help you.
They will contact media on your behalf and send press releases
introducing you and your book to the world. If you want, you can also
do a book signing. How fun an event would that be!
I can see it now.

flood

Introducing...

As for life in this matrix system,
I resigned from my job. I could not handle it more than three weeks.
Yuck-y.
I'm writing for a newspaper and I'm awesome.
I'm going to get a doctorate degree.
I need to maintain family status, it is their wish, and I love to learn.
What of status anyway?

As for my soul...
Sacred, I tell not.

The 'Arab-American', more Arab than American,
more Human than both.

I leave you with this...

I'm there over here.
When your spirit feels like crying
I'm here to help you cry.
When the world becomes just too much.
I'm here to hold it down.
When you suffer, too ill to move
I'll be here to bring you back to good.

To have been able to wrap myself in your voice...
It should have been awesomely cozy. For the moment,
Thank you for the attempt. Charming, really.

Jehan

catastrophes.

For The Sake Of It

Just out of curiosity…
1. Why didn't you write and call?
2. Why do you want me where you are?
3. You said, "I've been selfish toward you." I'm sure you knew that you
    were being selfish toward me as you were being selfish toward me.
    So, why didn't you stop being selfish toward me? You're not a child,
    you're rather refined, So?

I'm rather sorry, but really,
I cannot digest half of the things you say. Whispers inside tell me so.
So, just answer the questions. Don't try to dodge them like you usually do.
It's not that clever you know.

Before you leave…

See

So here we are like butterflies flying into change.
Here we are. All of us. Together.
Wow.
Life's mysteries.
Love. Isn't this the sacredness of it all?

She, tearing out of her confinement and flying free.

Fly like the butterfly God made you to be.

Peace, love and happiness on your journey home…
Your journey to happiness and well-being.

At this moment I would like each one of you
To share the happiest moment you've had
While intertwining with her being.
How shaking are memories when they make you cry.
Shake yourselves. Watch yourselves.

how

Black Crows

Black Crows were screaming today,
Exciting to hear.
What do they scream about?
It sounds as though they're angry.
What are they angered by?
Maybe it's the telephone wires that block their flight.
Could it be the large windows they crash into at night?
What if they're upset because somebody has taken their trees?
It's probably the pollution they sip from the sea.

Reality...
Forget the heartache they give you.
The fluffy clouds will save you.
Black Crows, don't scream anymore.
Fly far from here, sail to far shores.
Turn your furious eyes into calm.
Leave madness, go to another realm.
Feel the warmth in the sunset's air.
Surrender your mind to places up there.
Keep your soul.
A happy place you will find.
Black Crows, don't cry.
Fly into another world and pain will subside.
A happy place you will find.
Black Crows, don't cry.
Fly into another world and pain will subside.

the sky

I Have Seen Reality

I have seen reality.
It is not within the entertainment industries
Nor the corporations and conglomerates.
It is not the money we use to buy material goods.
It's not the societal norms considered important.
It is not the law of right and wrong,
Not Islam's Dogma,
Nor Christianity's Cross.

Oh, I have danced with reality
And tasted the sweetness,
Smelled scents of floral,
Danced until blissful and
Soared freely until the
Chains became undone.

Then, by His grace
Upon the Beloved I fell and
Passion of passions…
Nothing of this world can ever take His place.
Forever we are beautiful.
Beauty is eternal.

then

Have you ever felt Heaven here and now?
I miss you, the energy of you.
And thank you for telling me about the movie.
It was great.
Israel is making everything miserable for us.
Habibi, "Don't feel sad. Please."
I voted in Jerusalem's poll this morning,
Left-hand-side column.
I hope it will help in blocking any further notions of war.

rains

A Lot

It's so terrible that something so wonderful
Such as a gift from God could be 'a lot'.
God writes people into our lives.
He leaves the rest of the journey up to us.

And so...

As delicious as I am to you, so you are to me.
The resilience in you is the resilience you will find in me, too.

I've been wanting to say this so now I am.
I was once called the Arab American.
Thank you for the compliment.
But I would smile more if you would see me as being
More Arab than American...more Human than both.

Anyway...

I'm excited to chit-chat and relax.
I need to show you the world through my eyes.
I want to see the world through yours.

And by the way...

It would be foolish of me to have expectations.
I never get my hopes up.

In order to believe in God you must believe in yourself.
Your soul must believe in itself in order to feel the presence
Of the essence of God in order to believe in God.

down

Thinking Aloud

True, I was dramatic but I blame you and your Monday "Good-bye."
It was not cool. So, I felt, I forgot, I became, I forgave myself.
He wanted me to.

I wouldn't say "stringing me along" on a normal basis. This is drama.
What I meant to say was, "I don't want you to send me an e-mail when
you think I have 'detached'. That's too late. You rob me of a bursting of
whimsical feelings."

As for "smiling more inside,"… as long as you are smiling…
but I want to be sure. I just care, tremendously.

I respect you very much. I look up to you.
I think you are fabulously put together, my fabulous…

As for you, I hope to see you as the next Prime Minister of a country
if you want to be. It will suit you all too well. If you want, I can be
your spokesperson…charming, active, intelligent, supportive,
first-ladylike…so people will vote for you.

Even the taxi cab driver liked you. It should have been documented.
Everybody likes you. Do you know what a powerful strength this is?
God, your strength. God, your power. Truly, Habibi.

showers

Good morning, Lovely.
I wonder how it feels in Jerusalem?
It is evening over here.
Just finished dinner.
Writing flowing thoughts.
Love to celebrate them…

To prevent

Unconditional Love

I once knew a man who was gentle, generous, kind and loved
unconditionally. He was the gift among gifts but no one approved
of him because he came from a different cultural background.

Through the pain and sorrow of a love I could never have I learned
that you do not have to share the same culture or background to be a
good person. I learned to love all people no matter where they are from
especially when they are gentle, generous, kind and love unconditionally.

It is through hardships, hurt and sorrow we learn most
and grow closer to God.

over-drying

Another One...

Here I am sitting on my bed of thoughts
As they flow through this river of mine.
How dare you interrupt my world!

I once met a lion,
A caged lion.
Caged within his thoughts
He looks so serene and beautiful
Yet so ferocious, courageous and strong.

Anyway Habibi, handsome, tantalizing freak of nature,
Hayat, Amore' ...

And

I love when our energies intertwine.
We get all mixed up somewhere in time.

I adore the taste of your body and mind.
I need to take care of that baby of mine.

I remember the fresh scent
Drifting all over and around.

Let's listen to the echoes of our sounds.

Sincerely yours,
Jehan

Adieu Cherri.

to feed

Finally A Smile

I love this surprise!
A smile swept across my face today.
As I thought of Jerusalem…
How it smells,
How fruity the fruits taste.
It makes one so happy to be in Jerusalem.
Well, why wouldn't one be?
It's the Holy Capital of the world for many
And Home for some!

Anyway Sweetness,
I shall not keep you for long.
Seek the unmarked lands and the ghettos of the places you travel.
Share words with beggars,
Drink coffee with strange natives,
Walk the walk that gangsters walk (don't go alone).
People walk, cars drive, laughter laughs, speaking speaks.
Sit back and listen to every sound
And be one with the entire world of Jerusalem.

the animals,

When the orange leaves fall upon the soiled holy earth
A new season is born.
When the white moon turns the yellow sky black
A new night is born.
A cycle of life.
Working together in constancy and equilibrium
And when our foot gently presses upon the plush green grass-
It doth tread upon holy earth.
The earth's soul and our soul are one in time

And to feed

Have you lived a life of strife my friend — Of melancholy,
Come...and live in freedom. Come, Come with me...
Where the light shines bright, Where the grass is green,
Where the leaves play and sing, Where the thunder rolls,
And there's kissing underneath mistletoes,
Where the body's soul sways to the rhythm of the beat till it's old...
Come, Come with me.

the trees.

Today was an invigorating, relaxing, yet exhilarating moment in time.
Today, I ran through the clouds.
Today I walked to the middle of an open field,
sat Indian-style on mother nature's dewy grass, looked into the sky,
envisioned myself in the presence of God and sang to him.
As I sang my prayer I smiled.
After I sang my prayer I told God that He is awesome.
After I told Him he was awesome, I screamed, "I love God"
only to hear it echo across the sky to the distant horizon.
I stood up and ran with my arms outstretched and my hands wide open.
I wanted to fly. But instead I felt the wind
smacking my cheeks making way for me
and inviting me into the world.

Jehan Saleh

Hence we breathe.

Trees

Quiet is of the mind. Serenity feels kind.
The Universe is a ribcage of His dimension,
A correlation, a reflection, a monument of Him.
Everything is unified, even the outside.
See the trees He gives so we breathe.
The trees create gardens for us to see.
See the glaciers melt down their mountainsides
Into rivers, into seas.
See the sky taking up our water
To prevent flood catastrophes.
See how the sky then rains down showers
To prevent over-drying
And to feed the animals,
And to feed the trees.
Hence we breathe.

CPSIA information can be obtained
at www.ICGtesting.com
Printed in the USA
LVOW03s2000251017
553708LV00004B/448/P